Navigating Change

Initiating Governance

Harold Ainsworth

Published by KDi Asia Pte Ltd

www.kdiasia.com
www.kdi-americas.com

ISBN:
978-981-11-0577-7

Table of Contents

Table of Figures

PREFACE

Audience

This thin book is for Senior Managers who need to implement effective corporate governance of investments in program and project initiatives and operate these governance guidelines. Our key focus is on governance of project investments to obtain the best value for the whole organization, not just the individual parts.

It is my hope that by reading this thin book, managers will gain greater understanding and more effective approaches to improve program and project investment governance in their organizations so that investment in projects are more regularly successful.

Acknowledgements

Appreciation to those who have helped review material for this book including my colleagues Andrew Gunn, Terry Quanborough, Tan Kim Leng, Dr. Joseph Teo and Dr. Nancy Harkrider.

CHAPTER 1

Introduction

"Corporate governance is concerned with holding the balance between economic and social goals and between individual and communal goals. The governance framework is there to encourage the efficient use of resources and equally to require accountability for the stewardship of those resources. The aim is to align as nearly as possible the interests of individuals, corporations and society." (Sir Adrian Cadbury, UK, Commission Report: Corporate Governance 1992)

The Challenge

Every day governments and private organizations commit considerable sums of money to new program and project investments which they believe will return positive results, whether these results are measured in terms of increased revenue and profits, or the achievement of a social benefit.

Following some of the corporate disasters of the 80s and 90s there has been an increasing focus on Corporate Governance to ensure that senior management protect the organizations assets and investments for the benefit of all shareholders and stakeholders. Today there are professional groups, and an increasing number of books and consultants advising on governance in all its forms. Boards and senior management of organizations of all types are much more aware today of their responsibilities in this area, in some cases because of regulatory compliance issues, with penalties for failure to comply.

What is Governance?

There are many definitions of Governance but this one comes from the Institute of Governance (http://iog.openconcept.ca/en/about-us/governance/governance-definition)

"Governance determines who has power, who makes decisions, how other players make their voice heard and how account is rendered."

The key issue here is about how <u>account is rendered</u> since it is about stewardship.

The word Governance is commonly used these days, and sometimes loosely, so to be clear we need to understand that governance is not doing the work but ensuring the appropriate processes, controls and measures are in place to provide the best outcome for the organization as a whole, and not the individual department or business unit. The table below may assist.

Governance	Management
Approve and prioritize investments to create business value	Set them up for delivery
Do right things (effectiveness)	Do things right (efficiency)
Monitor overall performance against business case	Provide information and review performance
Ensure appropriate practices in place to manage investments	Validate information and make decisions about investments delivery
Ensure appropriate structures and accountabilities are in place	Arrange structures and for processes to be developed
Ensure appropriate support is in place	Provide support to programs and projects
Ensure processes are in place	Manage the process
Ensure business risks are considered and minimized	Determine, assess and manage risks

However, in reality when we look at governance of program and project investments, the term is mostly used to apply to those management oversight groups such as steering committees, program and project boards, control groups etc. responsible for providing direction to and reviewing performance of the actual programs and projects. To that extent some of their activities may begin to fall into the management column on page 2. It is very important however that they do not micro-manage program and project managers as that is not their role.

Principles

The Governance Institute of Australia (2015) has recently issued a publication called *Guidelines: Whole-of-organization Governance* and at the beginning of the publication indicates four key components which are:

- Transparency

- Accountability

- Stewardship

- Integrity

We will come across these components regularly as we progress through this book. Their booklet also mentions the importance of culture as *"Organizations have a culture – the question for boards and management is whether the culture is known and understood and whether the actual culture (the lived culture) represents the necessary and desired culture".* Culture is another important aspect that we will also mention later.

Project Governance

Our focus is on governance in relation to investments in programs and projects that are a subset of the overall corporate governance, because it is about ensuring the success of these investments to provide the planned benefits to the organization. The track record of success with project investments has not always been positive, whether it is in infrastructure, products, services or new technologies. The table below shows the difference between Governance and Management at a program or project level.

Project Governance	Project Management
• Approving the Business Case justification for the project investment. • Approving project plans for delivery. • Reviewing performance reports, and resolving issues escalated for decision, and deciding if the investment should continue. • Taking appropriate actions to ensure that the planned business value is achieved. • Holding people accountable for performance.	• Planning the activities required to produce the envisaged capability and outcomes. • Day to day management of the resources, budget, schedule, risks to produce the planned deliverables and outcomes. • Reporting on progress against plan around scope, time, cost, quality, and risk. Also if outcomes and benefits are still achievable. • Producing the deliverables.

There are two main factors to consider. Firstly, in the last 30 years there has been considerable attention given to improving the way we manage projects through improved methods and procedures, techniques, more sophisticated tools and abundant training to improve the capability of those involved. The number of certified or accredited Project Managers is rapidly increasing around the world. While we have seen improvements in many ways, it has now plateaued and more investment and improvement is not providing the appropriate level of returns.

This has led to a recognition that the second factor is how project investments are governed. Organizations that are more mature with project governance have a higher rate of success with their projects. (Knapp, 2011). Common problems that have been identified from many sources are:

- Critical decisions being delegated to managers with no authority;

- Lack of understanding of their roles and responsibilities of those involved as Sponsors or members of Governance bodies;

- A belief that when the project delivers the outputs the benefits will automatically flow;

- Decisions made on poor quality information. This applies to plans which can have unrealistic expectations, little understanding of the downside risk, or the full scope of work required to achieve outcomes including potential organizational change;

- Monitoring of performance where the information provided is inaccurate, lacks coverage and consistency, or is late;

- Minimal accountability for achieving outcomes.

Various recommendations have been made about how to improve the competency of senior management involved in project governance including:

- Awareness workshops for senior management about their roles and responsibilities;

- Support and mentoring in this role;

- Induction packs to explain the role;

- Training in project management;

- Some form of certification in order to undertake the role (personally I believe this is never going to happen and is not necessary, but it has been suggested).

While I would support the first three of the above list I do not believe the last two items are either desirable or necessary. It is not education in project management that is necessary for senior management but knowledge on how to perform the governance role and what constitutes good project practices so they know what to look for. In other words what questions do I need to ask to be satisfied that the right procedures have been followed, sensible results derived, and competent people involved. The purpose of this thin book is to provide that level of assistance to make your governance role more effective and satisfying.

Governance at Different Levels

As we will see later there are two terms used in relation to governance at this level:

- Governance of Projects which relates to the governance of all of the programs and projects in the organization's portfolio, and we cover this separately in Chapter 3;

- And Project Governance that refers to the governance groups that provide oversight to the individual programs and or projects.

For project investments there are three different levels, portfolio, program and project although in many organizations it is only two levels, as Programs are not currently used. To explain these terms the following diagram may assist. (Thorp, 2003)

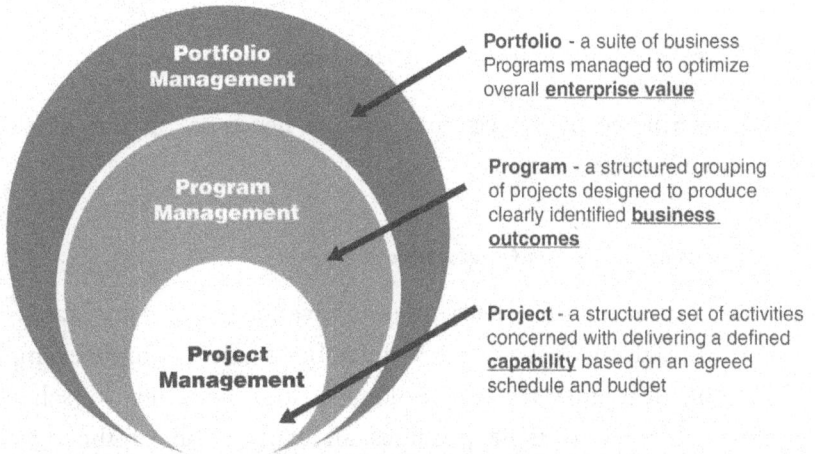

Figure 1 - Portfolio Program and Project Relationship Model

The table below explains the purpose of each level.

Level	Focus
Portfolio	The portfolio needs to consider optimizing value for the organization overall, which is challenging since various parts of the organization need to work together to do this and not in organizational silos which often happens.
Program	Focus on business outcomes that will lead to benefits and value to the organization, and is usually accompanied by changes in how the organization and its people operate. Without these changes the capability delivered by the project may not be effectively utilized.
Project	Delivery of certain capabilities with a focus on schedule and budget. There is a tendency today to also expect the project to deliver the organizational changes mentioned under programs above, but it often does not occur and is mostly more appropriate at the Program level.

More later on the focus of each of these components.

Governance of project investments needs to operate at all of the three levels above.

Example of Program Compared to a Project

My book in this series titled "Advancing Program Management" deals with this issue in more detail but I offer a simple example here to be clear since the terminology is often used very loosely in some instances. This table provides an explanation of the differences. Here is an example.

An organization is thinking about implementing a Customer Relationship Management (CRM) System. A computer vendor has been talking to the company's CIO about purchasing their CRM computer application software and the CIO has then spoken with the marketing department who believes it is a good idea. They recognize there is work involved in installing the CRM system and undertaking some training for the staff that will need to use it. You could look at this as two projects or a single project involving both technology and user training. However, in reality it is a program of work that involves more than this. Research shows that to be effective and obtain the desired outcomes (which is usually about customer retention and the customers purchasing more of the organization's products or services) they will also need to:

- Understand their customer base, who they are and what their profile and interests are;

- Look at the company's products and services to see whether they match the customer's profiles and interests, and determine any changes;

- Review the organization's processes that deliver these products and services;

- Understand the customer value chain;

- Review the organization structure to see if that needs any change;

- Undertake training for the staff in the new application software;

- Analyze if there is any old data that needs to be updated or migrated for the new system to be effective, and plan for this work;

- Plan the relevant marketing campaign;

- Also understand all of the changes required of the organization, including people's behaviors to make the above effective, and develop plans for it.

So effectively a CRM program is not about technology but a whole of organization approach to customer relationship including many of the facets on page 9. If they are not all adequately managed and coordinated the business outcomes will not be achieved. So effectively there are a number of projects that implement the actions on page 9 and are related but are managed together as a program of work to produce beneficial outcomes for the organization. Each of the projects focus on delivering specific capabilities and the program ensures that these capabilities are combined and exploited to produce outcomes and benefits.

Focus on Cost versus Value

Governance should focus on value at all times, and while this is easy to say it is often much harder to do. We understand costs better than we do benefits, since some of the benefits may initially be intangible, however they are still necessary to produce the tangible benefits. Also much of the costs are incurred in the initial stages but the benefits will tend to occur over a longer period of time. However, today there is a strong focus on TCO (total cost of ownership) that implies that all future operating costs need to be included in the equation. Sometimes future costs can even outweigh the initial setup costs. With purchase of application software there is usually a 20% maintenance fee each year that means in 5 years you have paid for the software again.

<u>Experience shows that there is a tendency to underestimate costs and to overstate the benefits</u>, particularly since some of the benefits involve significant assumptions. I have seen this situation as a consultant to a financial organization where benefits included in business cases included:

- Retain market share or customers (highly desirable but often difficult to quantify precisely);

- Increased revenue from customers (which ones, what products or services, and how much?).

Just as the assumptions behind the costs need to be probed carefully, so must the assumptions behind the benefits. Many commercial organizations will put great emphasis on various financial criteria such as NPV (net present value which uses a discount rate for future cash flows) or ROI (return on investment) etc. but all of them are only as useful as the underlying data used in the calculations. The "garbage in garbage out" syndrome is still alive and well today.

Some may even use more sophisticated modeling techniques such as Monte Carlo, but if you do not understand how it works, and its advantages and limitations, then it simply becomes a black box and you can be led astray by apparent sophistication. In many cases high priority projects are fairly obvious as are low priority ones, but the appropriate modeling techniques used correctly can help to sort out those competing ones in the middle that are not so clear cut and subject to a lot of interesting claims about what benefits they will deliver.

We usually do some level of risk analysis on delivery and especially on the time (schedule) and cost (budget) figures but rarely is there analysis on the risk to achieving the benefits, however this aspect should be given the same attention and rigor, and especially by those approving the investment. Value may be in the form of monetary measures or in the case of a government agency fulfillment of their objectives and mandate. The danger is that if we focus only on tangible monetary benefits then there is evidence to show that numbers to justify the investment can and will be manipulated to show a positive outcome. (The reason for the many comments made partly in jest about business cases being used to have the project funding approved and then you can ignore the promised returns since no one will check).

Framework

The author's Governance diagram, as used in the KDiAsia Governance Workshops, is shown on the next page depicting the areas of focus that are necessary to ensure project investments deliver value to the organization.

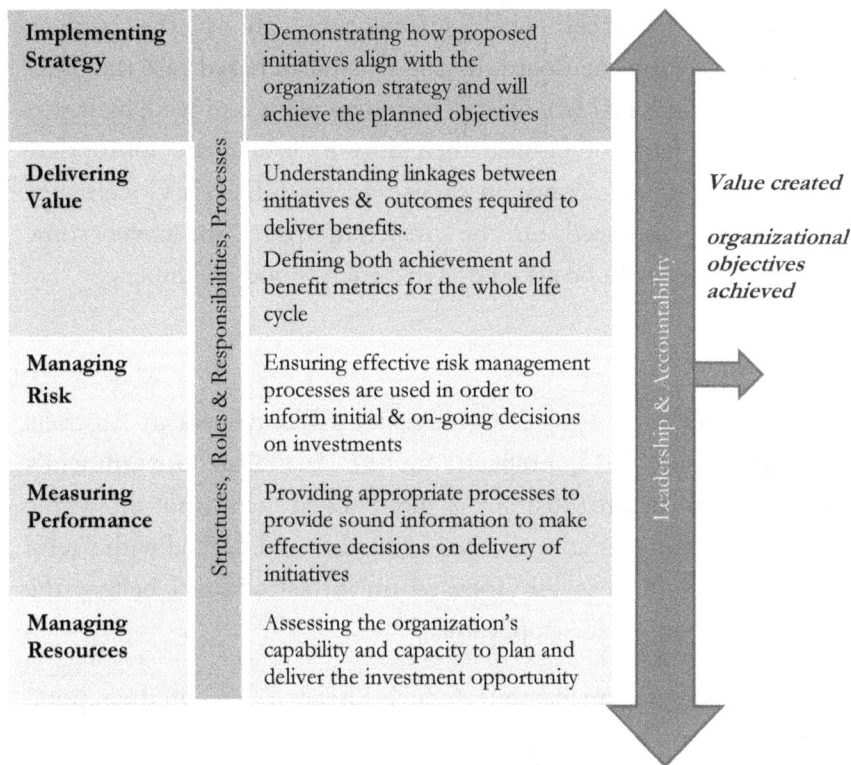

| Implementing Strategy | | Demonstrating how proposed initiatives align with the organization strategy and will achieve the planned objectives | | |

Figure 2 - Proposed Governance Model for Program & Project Investments

As well as these areas of focus, there is a need for appropriate structures, clear roles and responsibilities, processes to be followed and, above all over all, leadership and accountability must be exercised. Without these two topics in the right hand arrow, governance is just not effective.

Case Studies

There are a number of public domain project failure cases where the Auditor-General's report noted governance as a major reason for failure. We will look at several of these cases later but the interesting aspect is that in two of the cases the CEO of the Government

Corporation withheld vital information about the project performance from the Board. In one Australian based case the CEO lost his job, and also two Board members were removed, as it was deemed they had not fulfilled their duty by asking the appropriate questions. Ignorance is not an excuse. In the KDiAsia Governance Framework referenced on the preceding page, we cover some suitable questions to be asked by Governance body members.

Recent Research

A recent report on Project Governance Effectiveness in Australia (Caravel Group, 2013) prepared for the Australian Government's agency Infrastructure Australia is summarized below, but the whole report is worth reading as it is only 30 pages and packed with useful insights. While it is mainly focused on infrastructure I believe the lessons are more widely applicable.

The Overarching conclusion is: (which I believe sums up the report very well!)

"From the charts above, it is clear that a major cause of project failure in Australia has its roots in Project Governance or lack thereof.

*It also appears that the delivery of Project Governance in Australia is generally **highly dysfunctional**. (emphasis theirs).*

Notwithstanding Caravel's (the authors) experiences expressed herein, the reader needs to bear in mind that it is the survey participants who are largely pointing the finger at themselves. And, they are generally very senior experienced project governance and project delivery people."

Here are some really interesting observations from the paper:

- P11 – 70 % of respondents believe project value should be an additional criteria for success beyond the traditional scope, time and cost;

- P12 – 60% of respondents attribute poor governance as the cause of project failure;

- P17 – The authors undertake some very initial modeling of the potential cost saving with better project governance. The annual figures for the economy overall are very significant, and you should access the report to view their findings.

Structure of this thin book is as follows:

Chapter 2 – some of the issues to be considered and necessary steps to set up for effective governance.

Chapter 3 – governance across the project lifecycle considering what issues need to be covered at each stage.

Chapter 4 – evaluating governance performance, both process and results.

Chapter 5 – challenges in implementing project investment governance in organizations.

Resources – references to sources.

Endnotes

- Caravel Group, (2013) "Review of Project Governance Effectiveness in Australia", Infrastructure Australia, March http://infrastructureaustralia.gov.au/policy-publications/publications/Project-Governance-Effectiveness-report-by-Caravel-Group-March-2013.aspx accessed 25/5/2016

- Governance Institute of Australia, (2015) *Guidelines: Whole-of-organization Governance*, available from: http://www.governanceinstitute.com.au/

- Knapp, Michael, (2011) *"Optimising project success – the missing piece"*, summarising the results of a major research project undertaken in the period 2005-2008 as part of a PhD thesis at Sydney Uni., Presentation to PMI Sydney Chapter, August

- Thorp, John, (2003) *"The Information Paradox Realizing the Business Benefits of Information Technology"*, McGraw Hill Ryerson, Toronto

---

CHAPTER 2

Setting Up for Governance

"Optimization of parts of the system results in sub-optimization of the system" – a key principle of Dr. W. Edwards Deming, a prolific writer in the fields of mathematical physics, statistics, and finally, management philosophy and probably best known as the quality management guru.

Introduction

In the first part of this chapter we cover some of the <u>key issues</u> that need to be considered when establishing Governance, such as ensuring capability, fostering collaboration, classifying project investment for appropriate levels of governance, and understanding the risk tolerance of the organization. Understanding these issues helps us to establish the appropriate structures and process for governance.

Then in the second part we cover <u>governance at each level</u> (portfolio, program and project), roles and responsibilities, structures and how Stage Gating helps to make Governance effective by imposing checkpoints that need to be passed in order to proceed. The idea being that when working effectively, Gating forces reevaluation of the investment and, if it should still proceed, will be based on its ability to deliver planned value to the organization.

Issues for Consideration

Alignment

As the quotation at the beginning of this chapter suggests, there is a strong tendency in organizations to focus on parts of the system and seek to improve them, without understanding how these various parts fit together to make the whole system. It is my contention that project management is just one part of a larger system for delivering value to the organization, and while it certainly needs improvement in many cases, we also have to look at the other elements, including program management, portfolio management, and especially governance, which is the focus of this thin book.

In considering project investments we need to ensure that proposals submitted by divisions, departments, business unit etc. of the organization are aligned to the overall objectives and strategies of the organization and are passed through the standard channel (not through some "back-door" approach) to ensure overall transparency and consistency. We need to understand any interdependencies between them and in some cases where several proposals are pursuing a particular strategy, combine them in a program of work to ensure the appropriate level of coordination across the organization. This may require that the program be managed at a corporate level rather than at the individual business unit level, otherwise value to the organization may be lessened in order to increase the value to the business unit. There are techniques to help map these connections between various initiatives and the organization's strategy such as Results Chains (Thorp, 2003), Business Value Maps (Ainsworth, 2009), and Strategy Maps (Kaplan & Norton, 2004).

When all of the project investments are considered as an enterprise portfolio there are often duplicated efforts discovered which could be minimized or suitably coordinated to improve the outcomes.

You may wonder why a business unit would pursue benefits to its own area rather than the organization, and the answer is simply how performance is assessed. For example in some organizations the Procurement Group is targeted with purchasing at the least possible cost, which they often pursue with great vigor, irrespective of whether the purchased goods or services are the best for the individual business unit. So either the individual business unit needs to have an overriding veto, or the performance criteria for the Procurement group needs to be multifaceted and not just about least cost of purchases but also operational performance in conjunction with the end user group who utilizes the purchased goods or service. Creating these broader based performance measures is harder but drives more organizational focused behavior.

Case Studies on Alignment

I recently came across a situation in an international project services company that had a significant contract in the Middle East, where the local office had the client contract but required two other parts of the organization to contribute towards its achievement. One group was responsible for manufacture and delivery to site, and another part of the organization in Australia took on the project management responsibility. Each of the three divisions of the corporation pursued their own goals to ensure they were paid for their goods and services in full, and the project was not well managed resulting in a loss to the organization overall. The company Board mandated that they set up an Enterprise Risk Management Committee and obtain external advice on their Project

Management capability. Our advice was that for large programs of work involving multiple divisions of the organization each division's KPIs need to be aligned at a corporate level to achieving the best for the program and organization overall and not for each of their individual contributing groups. Aligning their respective KPIs would drive greater collaboration.

For a number of years I worked in a large multinational organization that had absorbed two other organizations over a number of years. In the office where I worked there was still three distinct subcultures operating, one as the initial organization as well as the two other companies it had absorbed. About five years later they were still not working as a single organization, which frustrated customers who had to deal with the various parts of the organization, and also it caused significant tensions between the silos. About one year after I left the organization there was a significant upheaval, with two new CEOs in short succession, and the majority of the senior management either moving or being moved on. It would be interesting to analyze how the company operates today and whether this massive change has finally created alignment and made it a single performing organization.

Despite being talked about for years the silo mentality is still alive and well in many organizations both large and small. Governance needs to operate for the whole organization not the individual parts.

Project Classification

It was common in the past for organizations to classify projects based on the cost of the project into three categories of small, medium and large. Each of these categories would require different levels of documentation and control, with small projects requiring an absolute minimum of project management. However, it has been recognized that the cost of the project is only one factor to be considered, and that projects should be classified more around a complexity and risk perspective.

The classification criteria could include any of the following:

- Size of project budget;

- Project duration and especially if there is an immovable deadline or long duration both of which raise the risk level;

- The number of the parties involved in the project at various stages, including external parties, with the larger number increasing the level of risk;

- Whether a new technology that has not been used before will be utilized on the project;

- Visibility of the outcomes in the public domain and the potential for reputation risk;

- The extent and level of business change required in the organization in order to implement the project outputs, with more change increasing the risk;

- Whether most of the project team will be co-located or if the project will be conducted across international boundaries which raises the level of risk;

- Any requirement for access to very specialized skills and their availability to meet the project timeframes.

Often there is a weighting applied to each of the criteria above, and then a rating for each of the items used, and an overall risk profile factor calculated. Depending on the number derived it will indicate whether the project is low, medium or high risk. For example a high-risk profile would require more detailed and comprehensive project management procedures, and also detailed reporting to management on a more regular basis. The risk rating should also indicate the level of Governance required which could include whether the project needed to pass through any, some or all of the Stage Gates (discussed later in this chapter) or if other independent reviews are required and when.

Understand the Problem First

In our natural desire to achieve as much as possible with the least resources and in the shortest timeframe, we often underestimate the problem and apply inappropriate solutions. I am sure that in hindsight you can think of many such examples. However, when we are in the situation ourselves we can be blinded by what seems a reasonable approach.

To paraphrase Albert Einstein *"If I were given an hour in which to solve a problem upon which my life depended, I would spend 40 minutes studying it, 15 minutes reviewing it and 5 minutes solving it."* The point is to apply more thinking about the problem before we rush to find solutions.

David Snowden and others (Snowden & Boone, 2007) have developed the diagram on the next page to help us understand the different problem spaces that we encounter. Sometimes a significant undertaking may have several components; that is parts of it may be simple and parts of it may be complicated or complex (see www.cognitive-edge.com for articles and videos).

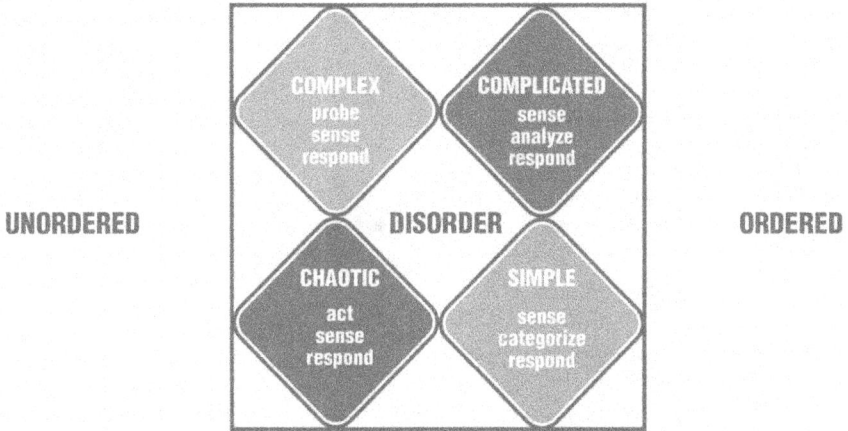

Figure 3 - The Cynefin Framework (Snowden & Boone, 2007)

Quote from Snowden & Boone (2007) - *"Truly adept leaders know not only how to identify the context they're working in but also how to change their behaviour to match"*

The table below and on the next page shows characteristics of each problem domain.

Simple	Repeating patterns & consistent events Clear cause & effect Right answer exists Fact based management	Complicated	Expert diagnosis required Cause-and-effect relationships discoverable but not immediately apparent to everyone: More than one right answer possible. Known unknowns Fact-based management

Complex	Flux & unpredictability No right answer – emergent patterns Need for creative & innovative approaches	**Chaotic**	High turbulence No clear cause effect relationships Unknowables Pattern based leadership

(Adapted from Snowden & Boone 2007)

Once we understand the problem space we are better able to discern the appropriate response, but even understanding the problem space is not instantaneous, especially for complex type problems where we need to look for patterns that can take some time to emerge and be understood.

So at a governance level we need to be aware whether sufficient time and effort has been spent on understanding the problem in order to develop the solution. The experts will believe so but we need to test this for ourselves, as the universe they see may be different than the larger one we need to operate in. This is also a good reason why serious option analysis should be undertaken as a part of the project life cycle activities and reviewed to help assist in our understanding the problem more and how it aligns to strategy implementation. You need to probe to ensure this analysis has occurred.

Capability to Perform

To obtain better outcomes from our investment in projects we need to consider raising the organizational capability and Terry Cooke-Davies (Cooke-Davies, 2015) reminds us that we need capability at three levels, and that none of the following is easy to create and maintain:

- Organizational capability covers:
    o Managing programs and projects portfolio, vs Business as Usual (BAU) operational capability and capacity;

    o Leveraging the organization's talent resources to perform portfolio management;

    o Understanding complexity and how to effectively respond;

    o Creating the right climate and behaviors (culture) to deliver programs and projects.

- Owner's capability covers:
    o Managing strategic initiatives – those significant initiatives that consume a lot of resources including management attention;

    o Governing and directing programs and projects involving executive sponsorship skills;

    o Managing and realizing benefits for investments.

- Project capability covers:
    o Effective project management to deliver projects.

Note the importance of culture above and it has been found that program and project investments perform better in a culture that supports openness, transparency and support (not blame) at all levels. Organizations need to be structured to accommodate not only BAU management, but also Program and Project Management investment, which cross silos in the organization. (As noted this is not easy to achieve except in organizations whose core activity involves performing projects – i.e. project services organizations.)

These capabilities rely on each other to perform. For example, project management needs the organization to manage the portfolio of programs and projects effectively, provide a suitable performing culture, and ensure that management involved in Governance are capable and committed to their roles and responsibilities.

The top-level governance needs to ensure that the organization has this capability at all levels to deliver the planned program and project investments. Attention to resourcing capacity is a requirement of Governance to ensure project investments delivers.

Collaboration

All of the preceding discussion assumes that there is effective collaboration in the organization. This topic is often talked about today but good practice is harder to find for many reasons. As noted elsewhere sometimes organizational systems and values do not encourage collaboration which requires a level of trust as it implies a certain loss of control, and many managers fear any loss of control. The more complex the situation then the less control we have, and the more we need to work together to share insights and solutions, and to monitor performance, since no individual by themselves can effectively manage the complex situations we face.

Collaboration will take various forms in organizations such as stakeholder workshops to discuss and agree on issues, and involving those performing the work in reviewing designs and plans for feasibility. (In construction projects this is typically called "constructability" by engaging those with detailed knowledge of how the work is actually performed to identify problems early). Governance must support effective collaboration to ensure results are achieved.

Risk Appetite or Tolerance

The Boards and senior management of organizations today are giving increasing attention to risk as part of governance. Some organizations have Enterprise Risk Management (ERM) functions and are documenting organization policies in relation to risk. They often talk about the risk appetite or tolerance of the organization for risk, which may vary in different parts of the organization. For example where it affects the safety of personnel there is zero tolerance, but there will be more tolerance for certain types of investments that incur risk. The organization may undertake certain program or project investments which are low risk because of their nature, but will also potentially invest in some more risky ventures involving new products and markets which they wish to engage in. So it is important for those involved in Governance groups to understand the overall organization policies towards risk so that they can make informed decisions when approving and monitoring the performance of program and project investments.

Roles, Structures and Gating Mechanisms

Governance at Each Level

Level: Portfolio	
Focus	**Issues to be considered**
The portfolio needs to consider optimizing value for the organization overall, which is challenging since various parts of the organization need to work together to do this and not in organizational silos which often happens.	What resources can we commit, both funding and people? How much change in the organization can we cope with at one time? What level of aggregated risk are we exposed to?

Level: Program	
Focus	**Issues to be considered**
Focus on business outcomes that will lead to benefits and value to the organization, and is usually accompanied by changes in how the organization and its people operate. Without these changes the capability delivered by the project may not be effective.	Are the planned benefits likely to be achieved? How will the organization change be managed? Are stakeholders fully committed, agreed on outcomes and the journey to arrive there? What strategic level risk are we exposed to?
Level: Project	
Focus	**Issues to be considered**
Delivery of certain capabilities with a focus on schedule and budget. There is a tendency today to also expect the project to deliver the organizational changes mentioned under programs above, but often does not occur.	Are we able to deliver the capability according to the approved plan? What support can the organization provide to the PM and team? Do we have the internal capability and capacity to manage this project? How will change be facilitated?

In some organization's the project and program focus above is often combined in projects since there is no program practice however there are very good reasons why this is not the best approach since there are two very different mindsets involved in delivering capability and delivering outcomes. Few managers can succeed at both, and when separated as above their attention is directed towards the appropriate issues to be managed. However, many do try to combine both which I believe accounts for some of the failures that we encounter. Programs are not just a large project, but are managed in a different way with a focus on the issues in the table above (see Chapter 1 Introduction for an example of a program). They require a different and more strategic business focused mindset. There is an interesting quote from a program manager that I think states the difference between program and project management, as "A key skill of good program managers has been described as 'managing the white space in between the projects', or all the activities that produce more than the sum of the parts." (Ward et al, 2013)

(The above issues are addressed in my forthcoming thin book in this series titled "Advancing Program Management.")

Roles in Governance

Following are the possible roles for governance groups.

Group	Responsibilities
Investment Management Committee (Portfolio Level) *Meets regularly - say quarterly*	Selects the portfolio of programs and projects. Monitors performance and makes changes as required. May operate the Stage Gates approvals or may delegate to another group who will ensure transparency and consistency.
The following would apply to each Program and Project (if not part of a program)	
Management / Steering Committee / Project Board / Project Control Group (Program or Project Governance Group) *Meets monthly usually*	Approval of plans and other key documents, review of progress, management decisions on policy type issues, especially escalation of matters that cannot be resolved by the team. Ensure all stakeholder interests are covered.

Group	Responsibilities
Reference Group (or other name) *Meets as required*	Designed to facilitate engagement of frontline staff that will be involved in working with the final outcomes, in order to collect their input, insights, feedback and contributions. Not a decision making body except at detail level and will be informed of performance and status.
Support offices	*Covered in more detail later*
Portfolio Management Office *Value management focus*	Collects the business case proposals and performs agreed analysis presenting the results to the Investment Management Committee so they can select the appropriate portfolio. Collects information on progress of programs and projects for analysis and presents to the Investment Management Committee for any decisions about changes to the portfolio. Communicates the results. Operates the stage gating process. (See below for more on stage gates)
Program Management Office *Delivery focus*	Provide support for the above groups and for the Program / Project Managers and the teams. Administration of centralized standard processes, templates and other resource material

The following are key roles that operate at governance level.

Role	Responsibility
Owner	The organization unit or Manager whose strategic or business plan creates the need for the Program / Project. • Provides overall direction and objectives for the program • Obtains or provides funding for the work
Sponsor	• Appoints the Program/ Project Manager • Ensures the Business Case is approved by Executive Management • Sets up and chairs Governance Group • Support the Program / Project Manager • Reports to the Executive Management about the progress of the Program/Project against the Business Case timeframes, budgets and benefits • Liaises with key business partners supporting the Program / Project

Possible Structures

Each organization will have its own structures in place and they will depend upon the size of the organization, the extent of the portfolio of programs and projects, and possibly the diversity of the business areas. The names of the various groups may also vary although they will have similar roles and responsibilities.

A possible sample approach follows:

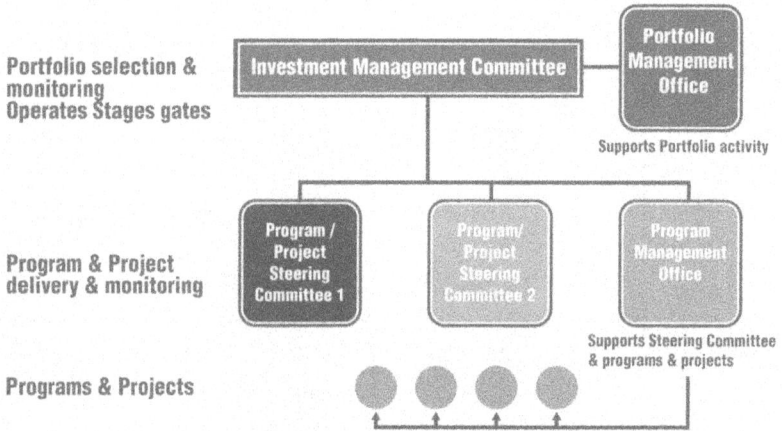

Figure 4 - Potential Governance Model

Effective Stage Gating

One of the mechanisms used for governance is to have gates or checkpoints at the end of each of the stages or phases of the project. The idea is that projects do not proceed pass the checkpoint without approval of a controlling body. In some instances funding is tied to each of the gates and will not be released until the project has satisfied the criteria for the gate. The aim is to ensure that projects do not spend a large amount of funding without adequate review both of progress to date and the likelihood of success at the end. There is a feeling in some organizations that these gates can become a "tick the box" exercise with insufficient rigor being applied. You can understand that if there are many projects it may seem considerable overhead to have every project assessed in detail. We discussed this under project classification earlier and suggested different levels depending on the risk profile of each project. Some may not need gating.

Establishing effective gating is difficult and will need top-level support since it disturbs the existing and often informal power structure and some manager's ability to manipulate the system to the business unit's advantage.

The following table suggests what might be assessed at each gate (at a very high level as there is usually a longer list of criteria).

Concept	Business Case	Detailed Plan
Determine if the concept is worth pursuing into a full Business Case	Sufficient information to justify proceeding with the project	Initial design to determine final estimates Detail on project delivery
Is there value in proceeding to a business case stage? How long? How much?	Cost / Benefit / Risk justification to proceed. Are stakeholders committed? Can value be achieved?	Detailed plans to implement – more accurate costs and benefits. Do we still proceed?
Can consume up to 12 to 20% of total cost		

Table continued on next page

Execution	Closure and Handover	Post Implementation Review
Execute according to the plan Make changes as required	Handover to operations or business users Project closure Knowledge capture	Benefits Realization review after some period of operation
Reporting against the plan, including cost & timeframe to complete. Do we continue? Will benefits be achieved?	Lessons Learned about delivery for future improvement	Ensure that benefits are being achieved Lessons Learned for future?

What is important about gating is not just whether the required documentation has been completed, which is sometimes given considerable focus, but a re-estimate of the cost and the benefits at that stage. We need to recognize that as more information is available our understanding of costs and estimates will change. Let us consider this simple example in the following table.

Approval or Funding Gate	Cost Estimate $ k	Benefits Estimate $ k	Duration Months	Comments
Concept	500	2,000	12	Order of Magnitude estimates

Approval or Funding Gate	Cost Estimate $ k	Benefits Estimate $ k	Duration Months	Comments
Business case	650	1,750	14	Budgetary estimate
Detailed plan	700	1,700	15	Definitive estimate
Execution – say 6 months duration	800	1,500	18	Forecast to complete. This should be reviewed as part of regular monitoring during the project

At each of the first three gates (concept, business case, detailed plan) it should be reviewed as to whether the project investments should proceed as the estimates are changing based on new information.

During execution there will be forecast to complete for cost and time, and at regular intervals, benefits should be also reviewed with their owners to see if they are still on track to be achieved. They may have increased or decreased. It is much harder during execution to decide to stop the project, since by that point, considerable investment has been made. However, it is still important to know what the final costs and benefits are likely to be. Benefits could have been severely curtailed due to some events which could not have been previously foreseen, such as a competitor launching a similar product or service and capturing considerable market share.

Also the requirements for the project may have changed due to government regulation or changes in current government objectives. Re-evaluation is an important role for governance and they may stop the investment, re-prioritize or even re-direct it to other goals depending on progress to date or changed circumstances.

Effective gating is a good mechanism to enable organizations to manage the value chain, to ensure that the value originally envisaged is maintained across the whole lifecycle of the program or project investment.

Up Front Spending

Some organizations will recognize in their gating system that a considerable portion of the project investment cost will be spent prior to any work being performed on the project deliverables. For example somewhere between 12 to 20% of the project budget will be spent in the concept and business case phase, and the detailed requirements specification and high-level design. See the diagram earlier in this chapter. If the project does not proceed past that point then normally this is a sunk cost that will not be recovered, unless it be can be reused elsewhere which is very unlikely and has been shown by history to be the case, as few projects are ever resurrected later.

Also the gating system will recognize that at each gate the accuracy of the estimates will vary, although I have seen instances where some organizations are pushing to have the business case estimates within a range of plus or minus 10% of the actual figure. This is very optimistic and mostly does not happen unless you have already performed the bulk of the design work which usually occurs after business case approval.

The following table summarizes the typical level of accuracy that you can expect at each stage. Obviously, we will not know the actual cost until the end of the project.

Stage	Type of estimate	Possible accuracy range	Comments
Concept	Order of magnitude	+ or – 100+%	Based on a broad outline of requirements and possible solution
Feasibility	Factored based on previous work or parametric information	+ or – 50%	Option analysis and recommend solution option
Business Case	Budgetary	+ or – 30%	Will require a reasonably detailed specifications and agreed approach to a solution
Detail Plan	Definitive	+ or – 10%	Can only be achieved once the bulk of the design work has been performed

Note the above ranges are acknowledged as being realistic by professional estimators but often not by other management who wish to believe otherwise, but nature cannot be fooled as they eventually find out! Sound estimates require reliable and detailed information!

However, I am sure that many skeptics will say that they have seen very few instances where the costs are never on the minus side, and very many where they are on the plus side of the above ranges. Governance groups need to understand the estimating life cycle on the preceding page and ensure that estimates provided are adequately supported and understood by all parties.

A Case Study in Failure of Governance (Based on Auditor General's Report).

- The project was a primary and secondary education digital learning platform for school students, parents and teacher use.

- In 2006 announced as a $60 million project.

- In 2013 it was in a "business as usual operational phase".

- Poorly planned and implemented and without a serious cost-benefits analysis.

- It has not delivered any of the main objectives it was funded for.

- Current best estimate of cost is $180 million but some costs were not properly recorded against it.

- Low usage by schools staff and students and declining.

- This situation may lead to its decommissioning.

- Three Business cases were prepared – first rejected, and second had failed tender process. Probability issues occurred over procurement.

- Received a Red rating for four of the five Government Gateway reviews, plus one Amber rating. The Gateway review recommendations were not addressed.

- A significant failure of Governance! And Gating did not work in this case!

Reflections

- What is the capability of your organization to perform and deliver value from their investments in projects? Consider the three capabilities; organizational, owners and project.

- Are there clear roles and responsibilities between the various parties and actors involved in both the governance and delivery of project initiatives? Do members of governance groups really understand their role and perform effectively?

- In your experience, is sufficient time given to understanding the problem before devising a solution? As part of your life cycle, do you have option analysis stage before proceeding to develop and justify the proposed solution? Is the option analysis a serious exercise and performed diligently?

- Do all project investments go through a well understood lifecycle with checks and balances at each stage including re-evaluation of the timeframes, costs and benefits as more information is available?

- Are project initiatives classified by risk profile and then the appropriate level of program, project and governance overheads applied or are all investment initiatives treated the same way?

Endnotes

- Ainsworth, H (2009) "Why Programs need to manage change to gain benefits", available from www.programvalue.com.au, accessed Nov 2015

- Cooke-Davies, TJ (2015) "Delivering strategy: What matters most, capability or maturity?", PMI Global Conference Proceedings, London, UK

- Kaplan, Robert S, & Norton David P, (2004), *Strategy Maps - Converting intangible assets intangible outcomes*, Harvard Business School, Boston

- Snowden, D J & Boone M E (2007) "A Leaders Framework for Decision Making", Harvard Business Review, Nov

- Thorp, John, (2003) "The Information Paradox Realizing the Business Benefits of Information Technology", McGraw Hill Ryerson, Toronto

- Ward, John et al (2013), "Beating the odds – the secrets of successful programmes", International Centre for Programme Management at Cranfield – http://www.som.cranfield.ac.uk/som/p19891/Research/Research-Centres/ICPM-Home/Publications/Whitepapers accessed 17/10/2013

CHAPTER 3

Governance Across the Project Lifecycle

"A 'no' uttered from deepest conviction is better and greater than a 'yes' merely uttered to please, or what is worse, to avoid trouble." – And *"You must be the change you wish to see in the world . . ."* – Mahatma Gandhi

Introduction

In Chapter 2 we looked at the project lifecycle that included phases such as concept, business case or justification, planning, execution, closure and handover, and post implementation review to assess performance. In this chapter we focus on what decisions need to be made at each of these points of time. They may seem repetitious but constant re-evaluation is necessary in light of additional information being available, and also performance to date.

In the first part of the chapter, we consider Governance of individual projects, and later governance of the whole portfolio of projects.

Project Lifecycle

A key principle of Governance is to be able to say "no" to some investments, prioritize all of them within the organizations capability and capacity, and to defer or stop those that are no longer relevant or likely to achieve their goals. It is extremely difficult to do this and often not performed well in organizations but something we must strive to improve in order to obtain better results.

We have broken the project investment lifecycle up into the following stages which are fairly typical of many organizations but do recognize that in some situations there may be additional stages or they may be called by other names. The names of the stages are not important but the underlying principles are essential

The stages are described in the following table.

Stage	Description
Concept	This is usually a short stage to identify the prospect at a high level and outline some broad analysis of cost, benefits, risk and business reasons for undertaking the Project. It is designed to ensure that business cases are not undertaken for frivolous ventures as the next stage is more costly to perform. It allows identification of the potential projects in the pipeline. Often approval for this stage gate is at Division Head level rather than a formal governance forum.
Business Case	Sometimes this can be broken into 2 stages, one where there is analysis performed to identify the best delivery options for the project, and then the full business case or justification is performed on the selected option. Otherwise it is combined in a single stage.
Plan	This is the stage where the business case is expanded into more detailed plans for execution. It is not always a separate stage depending on the level of detail required at the business case stage above.
Execute	Typically checks conducted during execution is regular (say monthly) reporting to a governance body although if the execution phase is extended for a long period there may be a formal review mandated at a key milestone.
Closure	The focus here is on how did the project perform against various performance measures, and capturing of lessons learned that could be used in the future to avoid repeating the same mistakes.

Stage	Description
PIRs	PIR refers to post- implementation reviews that are usually conducted 6 months or more after implementation to check whether the benefits have been achieved. Organizations are often not consistent in performing these reviews since the program or project team has disbanded and no one is tasked with undertaking the work. Also at times, there is a desire to cover up the known fact that the benefits have not been achieved. If these are not conducted we will never learn what the weaknesses are in the overall system and how they can be improved.

As discussed under Project Classification in Chapter 2, small or less risky projects may not necessarily be subject to all of these stages, or the approval to allow the project to pass from one stage to another maybe passed to a senior manager in the organization who has the delegated authority.

For each stage in the next table, we consider, as per our governance model in Chapter 1, and where relevant, the issues of:

- Alignment

- Value

- Risk

- Resources

- Performance

Also we identify two levels here – the portfolio governance view and the project/program level view. The portfolio view is dealt with at the end of this chapter.

Project Governance

As discussed earlier Project Governance covers the governance of individual programs and projects as compared to Governance of Projects.

Concept Stage

In some organizations, passing this gate is at the discretion of the divisional head since some or all of the funding or resources for the business case stage needs to be supplied from their operational budgets. However, the operation of this stage must be reviewed occasionally for effectiveness.

Concept Stage
Individual initiative (project or program) focus
• What is the business issue we are seeking to resolve?
• Is it worth investing more money and resources into further investigation of this opportunity or problem?
• What is the time & cost estimate of the next phase?
• Are the risks manageable?
• Is there likely to be business value in pursuing it based on rough order of magnitude cost / benefit analysis?
• Is the proposal heavily aligned with strategy or is it more business as usual approach?
• Are suitable resources available to prepare a business case?

Business Case or Justification Stage

The business or justification case prepared for undertaking the project investment can be a lengthy and costly exercise in its own right and should be managed as a project. In some organizations the project manager will manage it, but that is not always the case. Sometimes towards the end of this stage the execution project managers become involved both to familiarize themselves with the project, but also to provide a sanity check on the plans being developed. This is essential if the team and manager of the business case activity do not have hands-on experience in project execution.

Also if we want the execution Project Manager to be accountable for delivery they must be able to validate the estimates provided. In some organizations if the project manager has not been involved in the early stages, at hand over to delivery after approval of the business case the execution Project Manager must agree to the key performance indicators of scope, time and cost before proceeding. There must be acceptance of what is proposed otherwise the Project Manager cannot be held accountable against estimates established by others.

| **Business Case Stage** |
| **Individual initiative (project or program) focus** |
| • How is alignment to organization strategy demonstrated? |
| • Do we understand the complexity of the undertaking and allowed for it (See notes in Chapter 2). |
| • What are the key risks and their plans for them to be managed *(see note below)* |
| • Have the risks to achieving the benefits been identified and managed? |
| • Are the key resources identified and available in the timeframes expected? |
| • Was an option analysis performed and why was this delivery option chosen? |
| • What is the proposed timeframe and contingency allowed? |
| • What is the proposed budget and contingency allowed? |
| • Does the cost-benefit analysis include total life cycle costs? |
| • What are the key assumptions behind costs and benefits estimates? |
| • How were the cost and benefits reviewed? |

Business Case Stage *(continued)*
Individual initiative (project or program) focus
• When will more detailed estimates be produced based on additional information? • Have the stakeholders committed to the achievement of investment outcomes in the planned timeframes? • What are the key success factors? • Do we have a suitably qualified and experienced Program or Project Manager to lead this work?

Note: See KDiAsia book in Navigating Change Series - "Managing Project Risk" This book also deals with handling risk in complex undertakings.

Plan Stage

If there is a separate stage prior to project execution following the business case, then the execution project manager manages it, and more detailed plans developed to ensure achievability. If the execution Project Manager has not been deeply involved in the business case they will need to review delivery plans, estimated time and cost.

Plan Stage
Individual initiative (project or program) focus
• Similar to the business case or justification document however, you would expect to find updated details on cost, benefits, schedules, risk, quality controls, resourcing, procurement and the project organization and stakeholders. • How will performance be measured? • Have contracts been let or firm quotes obtained from suppliers or contractors? • As the next stage is execution it would be expected that specific information would be available to allow the project to move quickly to startup mode.

Execution Stage

Projects rarely proceed according to plan and there will be corrections necessary, and in some cases even a change of direction if external events to the project or program change the environment or the reason for the project investment in the first place. In some cases it may be necessary to reassess the business case in the light of changed circumstances, although few organizations even though they acknowledge the need, will do this in practice. If changes are required the project baseline of scope, time and cost needs to be changed with appropriate approvals to reflect the new situation.

Execute Stage
Individual initiative (project or program) focus
• Regular reporting to the appropriate governance forum on a range of indicators (see note below on 5 that can be used). • At a program level they will need additional indicators (also see below). • How accurate is the forecasting, and how do you know? For example has it been independently verified? (Or in some organizations the project managers performance KPI's includes the accuracy of their forecasting, which can be checked at the end of the project).

Governance bodies will only be effective if the right people attend, that is those with requisite authority and a vested interest in the project or program. The group should not be too large. I have heard of steering committees consisting of 20 to 30 people, which is absolutely unmanageable. Seven to ten members are sufficient.

It is important at this stage not to overload governance bodies with too much information so reporting should be concise and accurate with an emphasis on what decisions are required by the governance body.

Attention should be given to those issues, which the Project Manager requires management direction on.

For programs that last for a longer duration they need to also consider changes in the internal or external environment that may require change to the program strategic objectives or outcomes. Nothing remains static for long.

Project Performance Indicators – Top 5

The advantage of the following table is it turns each of the 5 key topics into a single number that if you understand the background to them provides very useful information. However, I do recognize that many projects will not be able to produce some of the metrics suggested so in the table following I provide an alternative but possibly less useful measures.

Area	Metric	Health Indicator	Use
Schedule	SPI (schedule performance index)	Indicates at what rate schedule progress is being achieved	Use to forecast overruns
Budget	CPI (cost performance index)	Indicates at what rate budget progress is being achieved	Use to forecast overruns
Risk	Usage of budget & Schedule Contingency reserve	Rate used should be lower than rate of progress through project	Use to forecast overruns

Area	Metric	Health Indicator	Use
Quality	Quality Milestones planned & achieved to date	Indicates if Quality Plan is being followed	May need to look further for potential quality issues
Scope	Number of changes / variations requested	Indicates scope volatility and possible change of direction	May need to review scope with stakeholders

Note: SPI and CPI above are indicators used in Earned Value Management, which unfortunately is not as widely used as it should be. Earned Value indicates, whether for the money spent, you are achieving what was planned to be achieved.

Alternative metrics are:

Area	Metric	Health Indicator
Schedule	• Planned progress to date • Actual progress to date • Planned and forecast at end	Indicates issues with achieving the schedule and its impact on the end date
Budget	• Planned spend to date • Actual spend to date • Planned and forecast spend at end.	Indicates issues with achieving budget and impact on the final project cost

Area	Metric	Health Indicator
Risk	Top 5 risks and their status.	With comparison to previous top 5 risks to identify persistent risks
Quality	Number of unresolved issues from the register. Unresolved issues from Quality Assurance reviews	Outstanding issues may indicate lack of decision-making. Indicates if Quality Plan is being followed
Scope	Number of changes / variations requested	Indicates scope volatility and possible change of direction. Possible need to review scope with stakeholders

Program Level Performance Indicators

Indicator	Purpose
Organizational Change Management	To assess through various means the progress and effectiveness of those activities designed to bring about change in the organization to enable adoption of the program and project outputs.
Benefits Tracking	A review of whether benefits are still on track to be achieved at the same level and in the time frame planned. This should be assessed in conjunction with the owner of each benefit who will be accountable for achieving it. Achievement and measurement of any planned intermediate outcomes.
Strategic Level Risk	Has the internal or external environment changed, requiring a rethink of direction? Performance of delivery partners.

The type of Program performance indicators used can change over the life of the program as they are more focused on the delivery of outcomes than delivery of capability.

Closure Stage

Often closure takes some time to complete since the project team has moved on and there was no one to perform this work. It is therefore essential that it be included in the project schedule and budget and is seen as an important activity before the team disperses. Trying to conduct a review after the team has dispersed or after a long waiting period means that we will lose the benefits of knowledge that will quickly dissipate over time. For a long duration project it is good to capture information and lessons on a regular basis since the passage of time again will cause a loss of important knowledge about events.

Some organizations will have procedures for closing projects that will cover both administrative work, contract closure activities, consolidation of key metrics into reports, and a meeting of the team and stakeholders to identify future improvements.

Closure Stage
Individual initiative (project or program) focus
• Is closure complete? (contracts, financial, staff reviews) • How did the project perform against the key indicators? • What key lessons did we learn for future improvement? • Are plans for a PIR (see below) in place? (When, who?)

Post-Implementation Review (PIR)

This stage is critical to assessing the performance of both the portfolio and the projects as to whether they have delivered on the planned business value. It will need to be undertaken sometime after implementation typically 6 or more months, and should be conducted as a learning exercise and not an attempt to blame any group or persons for failure, otherwise there will be minimum cooperation and useful outcomes. There may be reasons beyond the control of the projects or programs for not achieving the outcomes desired.

It is possible that not all project investment will undertake a PIR, however significant investments should perform one, and also a selection of other project investments to ensure the system works as expected. This review is best performed at a program level.

Stage	Individual initiative (project or program) focus
PIRs	At closure stage plans should be laid as to when this PIR to occur, and who to perform. When conducted report back to both project governance forum members and to Investment Management Committee. Follow up will be required since it will be some time in future and there may be political pressure to avoid conducting the review for a number of embarrassing reasons.

Portfolio Governance

As discussed earlier Governance of Projects relates to the organization's portfolio or programs and projects.

At a portfolio level we are dealing with all of the organizations programs and projects and a more strategic view is required. The managers involved will be very senior and form the Investment

Management Committee and the decisions will be very critical for the organization's health and future.

Stage	Portfolio or Overall View
Concept	The Portfolio Management Office would record the proposal in the register for visibility of initiatives in the pipeline.
Business Case (maybe split into 2 stages for feasibility and also business case)	Should some of the proposed projects be joined together into a program to obtain more coordination and synergy? Prioritize business cases based on the agreed criteria which may include alignment, risk, value (benefits less cost). Ensure there are sufficient funds and people and other resources available to meet the selected portfolio. Have we retained some funds in a management reserve to meet unexpected events? Can we manage the extent of organizational change implied by all the program and projects? Does the portfolio represent a sound balance between risk and reward for the whole organization? (Not too many high or low risks – what is aggregated risk level of all the project investments?) Are all of the proposed projects included in the portfolio, or are some not included or hidden from view (which defeats the goal of achieving transparency). Does the portfolio represent a good balance between maintain the business type investments and new initiatives to grow and transform the business?
Plan	It is unlikely at a portfolio level to review the plan separately from the business case but might occur for larger or more risky initiatives

Stage	Portfolio or Overall View
Execute	Portfolio monitoring may occur quarterly or monthly in some cases. A summary of the key indicators (time, cost, quality & scope) for each program or project to be provided but must also include cost/benefit (value) and organizational change performance indicators to keep the focus on achieving business outcomes and value. Organization change metrics are more qualitative and could for example measure acceptance of the need for change, and engagement of staff and capability built to date through training and other means. There may be changes required to the pace, direction or even closure of certain programs or projects that are not performing as planned, or their needs have changed.
Closure	Feedback on key lesson learned across the portfolio and what has been implemented to improve these situations.
PIRs	Feedback on benefits performance of programs and of the whole portfolio and also what lessons we have learned to improve the system. When will these improvements be made?

The diagram on page 56 is taken from Management of Portfolios (OGC, 2011) and shows two cycles. One of these is concerned about the <u>definition of the portfolio</u> where management decides on the "collection of change initiatives that will deliver the greatest contribution to the strategic objectives, subject to consideration of risk/achievability, resource constraints and cost/affordability." The other <u>portfolio delivery</u> cycle is about "successful implementation of the planned change initiatives as agreed in the portfolio strategy and delivery plan, while also ensuring that the portfolio adapts to changes in the strategic objectives, project and program delivery and lessons learned." (OGC, 2011)

The interesting link between this is _organizational energy_ that would include elements such as:

- "Senior management commitment, communication and motivation;

- A mutual and shared desire to succeed based on effective employee engagement;

- Effective governance with the appropriate level of bureaucracy;

- Culture and behaviors reflective of a focus on the overall good and success of the organization rather than individual or silo-based interest."

I believe the above expresses very well the role of Governance in ensuring the organizational energy is effectively used. This topic also relates to the organizational culture issue mentioned earlier. Note again the emphasis here on overall organizational success not just siloes in the organization.

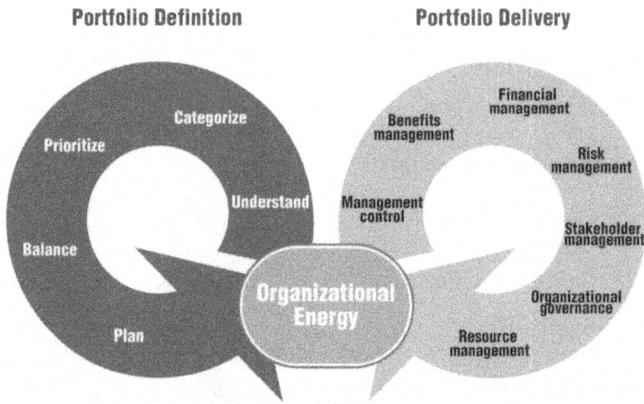

Figure 5 - Portfolio Management Cycle (OGC, 2011)

Case Study

I was involved for a period in a large program of business change in a government agency, with significant change impacts on the work of staff and management. There was a lot of dedicated effort occurring and when I joined I identified a number of serious omissions.

- The program had not been adequately thought through and the full extent of change understood from the start. There was not a clear understanding of how the components combined to produce the outcomes. So we developed an outcomes map to facilitate this thinking. (See Chapter 2 under Alignment section for references on mapping techniques).

- There was no change management plan and an assumption that everyone would just accept the change automatically, which was certainly not the case as some resistance was noted. We arranged for this plan to be developed.

- There was no adequate forum for discussion and resolution of the complex issues involved among the senior executives who were being forced to work in silos due to isolationist behavior of one of them. At a late stage, some changes were made to remove several work streams from this senior manager and to have other senior managers oversee them. We established a forum to facilitate issue resolution among senior managers.

- Poor leadership at a very senior level in the organization allowed this isolationist behavior on the part of one senior executive to continue and disrupt the program. Poor Sponsorship behavior.

- The focus was entirely on deliverables or outputs and not on outcome involving changed practices and behaviors leading to the reduction in processing times for their work packages. This is what the program was funded to do by the Government.

- There was insufficient visible performance KPI's to ensure the necessary level of commitment by all the senior executives.

- While some of our actions above would assist I still felt that the systemic issues were not being adequately addressed due to a lack of effective leadership and this would take more time to resolve.

All of the above issues we have covered in this book by showing they are part of Governance, not doing the work but rather ensuring the processes, systems, and controls are all in place and a supportive organization culture exists to enable outcomes to be achieved.

Reflections

- Are there appropriate checkpoints such as stage Gates at various times in the project lifecycle? Are these checkpoints effective in ensuring projects do not proceed if not viable?

- Is the health of the portfolio constantly managed and appropriate actions taken to redirect, cancel or re-prioritize project investments in accordance with current information? Are these decisions effectively communicated to all involved?

- Do governance groups effectively develop and utilize the "organizational energy" to deliver the portfolio of project investments?

- How does your Governance bodies assure themselves that the estimates provided about time, cost and benefits are realistic and based on the current level of information available, and not manufactured to gain funding approval?

- Is there appropriate leadership to make governance work effectively in your organization? If so where does this come from, and if not where should it come from?

Endnotes

- Office of Government Commerce (OGC) (2011) *Management of Portfolios,* The Stationery Office, Norwich
- Harold Ainsworth (2016) Managing Project Risk – for managers who want to ensure value from program and project investments by using smart risk management practices, KDiAsia, Singapore

CHAPTER 4

Governance Performance

"Governance and leadership are the yin and the yang of successful organizations. If you have leadership without governance you risk tyranny, fraud and personal fiefdoms. If you have governance without leadership you risk atrophy, bureaucracy and indifference." – Mark Goyder (Director of Tomorrow's Company)

Introduction

To measure performance of governance we need to look at two aspects:

- How is the process working?

- Is it delivering results in terms of value to the organization?

If the process is working well then it should be producing results, but it is worth checking both criteria.

In terms of process in this chapter we look at:

- Does accountability work effectively?

- Are Governance group members competent to fulfill their roles?

- Is Governance embedded in the culture so that it is not an add-on but a normal part of the way we work?

- The use of independent assessment to uncover issues that may not be recognized or at least discussed internally.

In terms of results we mention the need to measure whether program and project investments deliver planned value for the organization, not individual department or divisions, and how that is honestly and realistically assessed.

Measure Performance

There are many facets to performance. Cost is only one factor and is given a lot of focus because it is relatively easy to measure. Obviously we will want to minimize the cost but it also needs to be considered in terms of the planned beneficial outcomes. It may be better in some circumstances to spend more money in order to gain greater benefits, so cost minimization is only part of the overall equation.

Some of the benefits will be quantitative and some will be qualitative, and often the qualitative benefits are necessary in order to achieve the quantitative. Such qualitative benefits are about creating capabilities that can be used to deliver quantitative benefits as outlined in the Balanced Scorecard approach by Kaplan & Norton (2004). Quantitative benefits may sometimes be expressed in monetary terms but not always. If you are working in a government agency, there are times when most of the benefits will not be expressed in monetary terms but in quantified social benefit terms. For example turnaround times for approvals, community consultation and engagement about decisions, transparency of process and information etc.

Implementation success is also important since it is possible to have a well-managed project but the transition to operations can be fraught with problems. The Heathrow Airport Terminal 5 is a classic example of this with a well-managed project until the cut over to operations that resulted in a disastrous chaos with numerous flight cancellations and problems with passenger's baggage. This caused considerable embarrassment and reputational damage to many parties.

In the past project success has typically been measured in terms of delivery to scope, time and cost. However, it is accepted these days that this "iron triangle", as it is called, is insufficient and we need more comprehensive success criteria such as:

- Quality (could also be covered as part of scope)

- People satisfaction; (team, stakeholders and even suppliers with how the project was managed)

- Environment and sustainability; (does not create problems for future generations)

- Health and safety; (no harm to those involved in any way)

- Social contribution; (does not pass unnecessary burden onto the community)

- Achievement of business value, however measured

How does your organizations governance performance rate in terms of achieving the above?

We need to seek optimization for the organization as a whole and not individual business units, since organizational silos still exist and because performance measures pursue their individual goals. For review, you may want to revisit Chapter 2.

Independent Assessment

An independent assessment by external parties can be beneficial, since in the process of collecting information, they are able to obtain useful insights from managers who may not be willing to share those observations with their peers. The consultants, by obtaining different viewpoints and analyzing the results, can obtain a sense of where the potential problems reside which may not necessarily surface publicly within the organization.

Chris Argyris (Argyris, 2000) talks about the idea that in organizations there are "undiscussables" as issues which are not publicly mentioned in the organization. Even the fact that there are "undiscussables" is not ever discussed. This is unfortunate since it means that these issues which are mostly root-cause problems simply remain and any action taken is treating the symptoms rather than the cause. I have worked in organizations where these "undiscussables" exist and I am sure that readers will have observed the same phenomena.

At some stage if the organization is to progress these difficult issues will need to be dealt with but it is a brave person who will break the taboo and raise them. Sometimes a new CEO coming into the organization will address the issue since they are not part of the historical legacy that created them.

Accountability

John Thorp talks about "activist accountability" (Thorp, 2003) which has the following seven conditions:

1. Clear mandate and scope

2. Sufficient authority and latitude to act

3. Requisite competence

4. Commensurate resources

5. Clear lines of accountability

6. Understanding of rights and obligations

7. Relevant performance measures

He also adds that there must be acceptance of the accountability by the person. I think the above list is very useful because we see situations where people are being held accountable without sufficient authority, competence, resources etc. If these conditions do not hold true we would be best not to accept accountability. It is important that those imposing accountability ensure the above conditions exist to confirm that accountability is effective in the organization: otherwise it can easily become an exercise in trying to avoid accountability by many and devious means.

Accountability has to be taken very seriously and not just in name. Performance measures must impact either their remuneration, bonus or even their tenure in the organization. Or at least there needs to be public awareness of the performance.

For example, I remember reading the story of a Police Commissioner in the USA who used to meet with his divisional heads to review their performance against agreed targets. There were always excuses as to why they had not met the targets and quite often they would blame other divisional heads for impacting their lack of performance. To overcome this he decided that these performance reviews would be held jointly with other divisional heads. Each divisional head needed to present to the group of their peers and the Police Commissioner on the performance of their division. This made it very difficult for them to be laying the blame on their peers who were present. Over time, performance improved since they were having to be accountable in front of their peers.

This provided an extra level of motivation to perform as agreed since there was nowhere to hide!

Accountability is often focused on business as usual results but less so for capital funded programs and projects. KPIs for spending on project investments must also be tied into the KPIs of divisional managers responsible for achieving the benefits from the investment.

Role Competency

It has been observed that in many situations people fulfilling sponsor roles or being members of governance bodies such as steering committees are not completely clear on their role, or the means to fulfilling it. Obviously they are looking for some assistance to guide them but it rarely exists. External parties can conduct internal training courses but it is necessary to overcome the perception of some managers who may feel this is not appropriate for a person in their position. There are very few public courses of this nature and then the problem is keeping the course relevant to people from a wide range of organizations at different levels of maturity. In-house tailored course such as offered by KDiAsia are a more effective learning approach.

Individual coaching by an external advisor is certainly a helpful way of raising capability, although it may need to be disguised so that it is less obvious as to what is occurring. Some organizations will provide induction packs to those undertaking a governance role, which is certainly better than nothing, but lacks the individual touch which many desire.

Another approach would be to have an external consultant sit on the stage gating forums to observe what is occurring and provide group and individual feedback to gating forum members on how the sessions can be improved. The consultants can even take an active role in the gating activity in order to provide a role model for some of the other participants, but it does need to be handled with sensitivity.

Managers who are responsible for governance need to make an honest assessment of their capability and, if lacking, seek assistance, as the role is so critical to good organizational performance.

KDiAsia offers workshops for senior managers in the governance activity conducted by very experienced consultants and trainers to help raise the level of capability in the organization.

Case Studies

The following case studies have been extracted from two Auditor-General's reports.

Type	Government-owned Water Utility
Failure to deliver	**Governance failure**
• Cost increased from $38.2 to $61 million when cancelled and estimated completion cost then was $135 million • Original timeframe of 20 months which increased to estimated 33 months before project cancelled • Lack of effective stakeholder engagement • No integrated schedule • Poor contract administration • Poor risk management	• Steering committee not effective • PM lacked sufficient experience, consultant recommended replacement but took some time to occur • Failure to report true status to the Board. CEO withheld information. • Business Case benefits not clear or monitored • Failed to implement recommendations of several external consulting reports • Technical Proof of Concept study planned but not utilized - meant to be checkpoint

Type	Government-owned Transport Corporation
Failure to deliver	Governance failure
• Cost increase from $210 to $463 million • Original timeframe of 3 years increased by 18 months for initial delivery with further delivery of 2/3 of the scope to come later • Good PM practices not applied • Scope changes not reflected in schedule & budget	• Lack of information supplied to Board • CEO placed himself in conflict of interest situation by acting in 2 roles – CEO of overall Corporation and also CEO of their subsidiary building the transport for the overall Corporation. • External Board Directors with domain experience removed early in project • Decision to launch project rushed • The whole project became a political decision not supported by sufficient analysis

While these cases may seem to be more significant initiatives, the same principles apply to smaller and less costly undertakings.

Another challenge that governance groups must face is to ensure that consultants do not end up in situations where there is a potential conflict of interest between serving their own organization and serving the client. This sometimes happens when the client or an organization does not feel they have sufficient competency to manage the consultants effectively and allow them to manage the whole project for the organization. It may require the client organization to engage another independent consultant to act as an advisor, even if on a part-time basis, to assist them to monitor the work of the first consultants who are performing the work.

Embed Governance in the Culture

Ultimately we want Governance to be embedded in the culture of the organization. By that I mean that it becomes *"just the way we do things around here"* and not something special or an add-on or afterthought. However, for many organizations this means some change in the way things are done, and we know this is not easy since *"it deals with the complexity of human interactions"* (Harkrider and Tan, 2013). This Facilitation Model demonstrates how the book and the workshops KDiAsia offers can assist your organization in planning and adopting the necessary changes in order to implement improved Governance. The book and the workshops KDiAsia conduct can assist your organization in planning and adopting the necessary changes in order to implement improved Governance.

People are drivers of change in an organization

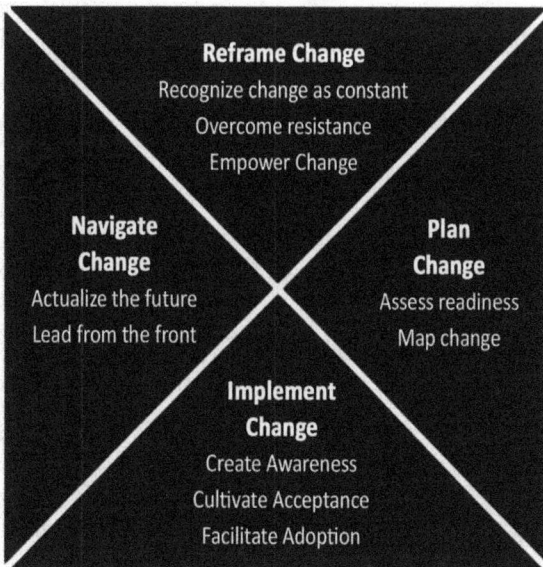

Reframe Change
Recognize change as constant
Overcome resistance
Empower Change

Navigate Change
Actualize the future
Lead from the front

Plan Change
Assess readiness
Map change

Implement Change
Create Awareness
Cultivate Acceptance
Facilitate Adoption

The leadership role changes in each phase of the model

Figure 6 - KDi's Change Facilitation Model

Resource (also see "Resources" at end of book)

ISACA (Information Systems Audit & Control Association) (www.isaca.org) are the body behind the IT Governance Institute (www.itgi.org) and the publishers of the COBIT framework that has evolved over the years into version 5. COBIT is used the assist IT groups implement sound IT Governance which is part of overall corporate governance. It is a comprehensive and well-established framework covering all aspects of IT, and has detailed implementation guidance available in various documents, so it is worth investigating. This book adopts the principles that support the governance of program and project investments according to the COBIT Framework, most of which can be applied to any investment in programs or projects.

There are 5 principles to COBIT (ISACA, 2012):

Principle 1: Meeting Stakeholder Needs – Enterprises exist to create value for their stakeholders by maintaining a balance between the realization of benefits and the optimization of risk and use of resources.

Principle 2: Covering the Enterprise End-to-end – COBIT 5 integrates governance of enterprise IT into enterprise governance.

Principle 3: Applying a Single, Integrated Framework – COBIT 5 aligns with other relevant standards and frameworks at a high level, and thus can serve as the overarching framework for governance and management of enterprise IT.

Principle 4: Enabling a Holistic Approach – Efficient and effective governance and management of enterprise IT require a holistic approach, taking into account several interacting components. COBIT 5 defines a set of enablers to support the implementation of a comprehensive governance and management system for enterprise IT. The COBIT 5 framework defines seven categories of enablers.

– Principles, Policies and Frameworks

– Processes

– Organizational Structures

– Culture, Ethics and Behavior

– Information

– Services, Infrastructure and Applications

– People, Skills and Competencies

Principle 5: Separating Governance from Management – The COBIT 5 framework makes a clear distinction between governance and management. These two disciplines encompass different types of activities, require different organizational structures and serve different purposes. (See Chapter 1 Introduction – "What is Governance" for more on distinguishing the roles).

Reflections

- Is accountability effective in your organization, so that managers who have the authority make decisions and pursue actions as good stewards in order to deliver benefits to the organization for investments placed in their care?

- Do senior managers responsible for governance in the organization understand their roles and believe they are fully competent to fulfill these roles and ensure that good practices are followed to enhance the chance of successful outcomes?

- Does the organization attempt in any way to measure the effectiveness of governance?

- What support does the organization provide to enable managers to be effective in their governance role?

Endnotes

- Argyris, Chris (2000) *Flawed advice and the Management trap - How managers can know when they're getting good advice and when they're not*, Oxford Press, NY.
- Harkrider, Nancy & Tan, Kim Leng (2013) *Leading Change that Matters – Making Adoption a Reality*, KDiAsia, Singapore
- ISACA, (2012), COBIT 5 - A Business Framework for Governance and Management of Enterprise IT, ISACA, Rolling Meadows, IL, USA
- Kaplan, Robert S, & Norton David P, (2004), *Strategy Maps - Converting intangible assets intangible outcomes*, Harvard Business School, Boston
- Thorp, John, (2003) *"The Information Paradox Realizing the Business Benefits of Information Technology"*, McGraw Hill Ryerson, Toronto

CHAPTER 5

Challenges in Implementing Program & Project Investment Governance

"Organizations need to practice qualitative corporate governance rather than quantitative governance thereby ensuring it is properly run." – And "You cannot legislate good behavior." – Mervyn King (Chairman: King Report on Corporate Governance)

Introduction

In this chapter we cover challenges in implementing project investment governance which include:

- Is it recognized as adding value or is it seen as another overhead?
- Good governance provides transparency and can easily disturb existing power structures in the organization and lead to opposition
- We can have too much Governance type controls – it needs to be aligned to size and risk profile of the project investment (not just project cost since a small project investment can have significant reputational risk to consider)

- Governance relies on a positive culture and good leadership
  that supports creation of value for the organization

These challenges can only be overcome by support from the Board
and senior management of the organization working together in a
collaborative manner. It is recognized that this is hard work that
requires leadership at both of these levels! Process and structure are
insufficient by themselves.

Value of Governance

The above quote tells us that we need to be able to assess the quality
of our governance and not be blinded by the quantity of it. As noted
earlier organizations implement stage gating on project investments
but it can simply be a "tick the box" exercise, which adds overheads
but creates minimum value. We need to consider the effectiveness
of governance and tune it as required.

The latest draft version of the King Report on Corporate
Governance (Institute of Directors, South Africa, 2016) summarizes
in principle 2.1 many of the concepts outlined in this book. *"The
governing body should lead the value creation process by appreciating that
strategy, risk and opportunity, performance and sustainable development are
inseparable elements".*

An appropriate balance is required based on sound judgment that
will be informed by objective information. All members of the
organization need to understand the purpose of governance and not
see it as simply additional overheads designed to make more work
for them. What is its value?

Good governance implies transparency in the process to select and
resource projects across the organization. It may upset the current

power structures in the organization where certain managers know how to "work the system" to obtain the funding for their projects over other business units or departments and divisions.

Similarly when PMO (Program Management Offices) or PfMO (Portfolio Management Offices) are created, they may also have the same effect, since typically these groups are about consistency and visibility of process, also about providing objective independent information to governance groups. Their work can bring to light instances where information has been manipulated or hidden, or whether processes and policy are being appropriately followed. Some of this may not be good news to certain managers who do not desire this level of transparency, but should be applauded by those managers who want to see the best outcomes for the organization overall.

Effective governance will also ensure that the organization does not rely on "heroes" to achieve outcomes, since these "heroes" can be in short supply, or have large egos that will distort the culture and values of the organization. Instead the organization should be able to rely on dedicated staff following appropriate processes with the suitable level of management control and accountability, which is a more sustainable approach.

There is a case study of an Australian financial institution that implemented a PMO to improve effectiveness of their projects (Dovey & Fenech, 2007). The PMO manager went about it the correct way and for a while was successful, however ultimately business managers felt that their power had been curtailed by the new processes adopted and lobbied the CEO to disband the PMO. Subsequently a significant project for the organization failed completely and the Board removed the CEO, and mandated that the PMO was re-established. This was a valuable lesson about power structures and the need for transparency.

A level of balance is required so that oversight is commensurate to the level of risk and that we do not waste resources on inappropriate control levels. I have seen this happen in a large organization which was out of control in terms of capital spending allocation and performance measurement, where they implemented stricter controls through a stage gating process and portfolio management offices. While there was considerable support in many parts of the organization for what they had implemented, there was also a widespread belief, when I interviewed managers at all levels that the process now needed to be tuned. The review and tuning suggested would seek to automate the process more and avoid duplication of effort, and also not apply the same level of rigor to all project investments, but rather depending on their significance and risk profile. Failures to make these changes would only cause loss of support from those in favor, and create more reasons for people to try and avoid using the system effectively.

Deal with the Real Issues

We need to be very careful that the time spent on Governance addresses the real issues, which is about delivering value for the organization and how that is managed. This will require a focus on all the factors including process, people, technology, structures, measures, culture and values. Culture and values as a necessary part of Governance is becoming more often talked about today. This thin book has endeavored to address the need to look at fixing systemic issues and not treating the symptoms. We have considered in our journey through this book examples such as performance measure that support organizational behavior rather than that of individual business units, and the processes and controls required to obtain realistic estimates rather than fanciful figures. So for Governance group members they need to ask themselves as to whether the organization's system and culture etc. supports the behaviors that deliver value. Too many focus on scope, time and cost measures and deliverables, to the exclusion of value criteria.

Questions on Governance

So let us conclude with some questions to consider about governance that you can ask about your organization and how it performs in each of these questions.

Topic	Questions to consider
Portfolio	• Are all investment opportunities included in the portfolio or do some bypass it? (It is possible to exclude some BAU type activities particularly if they are funded out of local budgets) • Have any projects being stopped, redirected or re-prioritized as a result of portfolio performance monitoring? • Do senior and Business Unit managers in the organization feel there is a transparent and open process for investment selection? • Is there a major focus within the portfolio on delivering business value from these investments? How is this evidenced?

Topic	Questions to consider
Programs	• Do programs monitor the environment for change and make suitable responses to any internal or external variations? • Are program managers ensuring effective coordination with other projects and programs and not micromanaging the projects? • Do programs have a continual focus on achieving the benefits and also ensuring the organizational change occurs? • Do programs that cross business unit boundaries have strong support from the BU managers involved? • Are program managers selected on the basis of their business acumen skills and strategic focus?
Projects	• Is there accurate, timely and comprehensive reporting that allow for effective decision-making? • How is project performance validated? • Are there organizational initiatives to build capability in delivering projects?
Governance	• Does the Governance group adopt the appropriate approach depending on the nature, risk or complexity of the investment initiative? • Is there an organization culture promoted that fully supports program and project delivery with transparency and accountability? • Are decisions made that recognize that new initiatives require considerable investment of resources and as such compete with BAU activities and a balance between their needs allowed for?

None of the above is easy but as discussed earlier Governance is about stewardship and requires diligence.

Capability

You may find it helpful to check back to Chapter 2 for the three levels of capability required in organizations from Terry Cooke-Davies (under *Capability to Perform* heading) in answering the above questions.

A useful starting point is to convene a workshop of the senior management to discuss the organization's governance capability and what is required to improve transparency, consistency and ensure the stewardship of resources for the benefit of stakeholders. A subset of this would be to focus on the governance of investments in new project initiatives. However, the owner's representatives, whether they are the Board of a corporation, or the Board of the government entity, or the Government Minister, should also be consulted to ensure that they believe that the organization has the appropriate level of governance capability to ensure effective stewardship. An independent assessment may assist, if handled with sensitivity, to determine the real level of capability compared to other organizations.

I have mentioned Leadership before in connection with governance (Chapter 1) but managers should be very careful of dismissing this as someone else's problem. There has been a strong drive in the literature over the years to distinguish between leadership and management roles. Henry Mintzberg in his book "Managing" (2011) analyzed the work of many managers and leaders that he was studying and found that it mostly was hard to distinguish between the two roles. Having been a senior manager myself on a number of occasions, I believe it has been absolutely necessary for me to demonstrate leadership as well as management. Senior managers involved in Governance also need to consider doing the same.

In the next section "Resources" we include a "case story" of different approaches a Governance body might adopt to problems with a Program or Project and analyze why some of these approaches might not be helpful and other more helpful. It might help you consider how your Governance groups operate and how effective they are and why.

Reflections

- Is the delivery and governance of project investments a sustainable approach that is repeatable and does not rely on heroes to deliver in a chaotic situation?

- Is there good transparency on how decisions are made about investment in projects so that all understand the criteria and reasons for these decisions?

- How effective is accountability for achieving the planned business outcomes from investments?

- Does the organization have a Program Management Office or Portfolio Management Office to support both governance and the delivery of the project investment?

- When was governance last improved?

Endnotes

- Dovey, K & Fenech, B (2007) "The role of enterprise logic in the failure of organizations to learn and transform – a case from the financial services industry", Management Learning, Nov, 38, 5, pg 573.
- Institute of Directors, South Africa (2016) Draft King IV Report on Corporate Governance, Institute of Directors, South Africa.
- Mintzberg, Henry (2011) *"Managing"*, Berrett-Koehler, SF

RESOURCES

References to standards and other sources

- The IT Governance Institute (www.itgi.org) has some useful papers on governance and although oriented towards information technology investments the principles can be more widely applied. The COBIT framework mentioned previously will also be found here.

- Governments in many countries have papers available on their Gating mechanisms. With Government Gating procedures there is often a lot of emphasis on procurement since most of the work is performed by outside organizations, which may not be the case with commercial organizations.

- The Canadian Government has a Centre for Excellence for Evaluation has some useful papers. The website is moving so try a search of internet for this site.

- Also there are numerous papers available from many Governments about the topics of Gating, Business cases for investments, Benefits Realization, Value management, Risk, and Project Management.

- The King Report on Corporate governance from South Africa offers a good understanding of principles and practice. The latest version is III (2009) and available from the Institute of Directors in South Africa.

- The UK Government has a number of well-known best practice guides on Governance issues – Prince2, Management of Portfolios, Managing Successful Programs, now commercially available from Axelos (www.axelos.com/best-practice-solutions)

- The Project Management Institute (PMI) has a Practice Guide on "Governance of Portfolios, Programs and Projects: A Practice Guide" published in 2016 - see www.pmi.org

- The Association of Project Managers (APM) in UK has a publication "Directing Change: A Guide to Governance of Project Management" 2011 - see www.apm.org.uk

A Case Story

This is not a case study in the normal sense of the word but is rather a combination of many situations I have come across, or shared with me by colleagues, including this one that illustrates some of the challenges of Governance.

What happens when projects and programs are not performing? There are a number of potential responses, some that are not very helpful, and some that are a better response but often harder to implement. So let us consider a program or project that is not performing as expected, which might include time frame extensions, significant increases to budget, quality issues, and, even more importantly, not achieving the outcomes that will ultimately contribute to business value. What responses from the Governance body might occur?

Not very helpful responses
1. A tendency to focus on the items that are not very important (we will call these trivia) since the real issues are much harder to deal with.   (*Comment* - This way Governance can be seen to be taking action, even if we are not sure of what the root cause is. However, it can create more delays that then can make the situation unable to be retrieved.)

2. A strong motivation to find somebody to blame. The first place is often to blame the Program or Project Manager, since these people are more expendable than senior management in the organization.

   (*Comment* - While it is sometimes appropriate to replace the Project Manager, and I have done this on many occasions, there are circumstances that are completely beyond the control of the Project Manager. Blame is often not a helpful approach to resolving the problem.)

3. "Escalation" or let us spend more money to fix the problem, since if we stop now it will look like we have wasted all the money spent to date.

   (*Comment* - This response represents a failure to recognize money spent as a sunk cost and let it go rather than waste even more money. Find the root cause before spending more money - see below.)

4. Can we hide the truth for longer in the hope that the problem will fix itself or go away, or I will have moved on by the time it is discovered?

   (*Comment* - In some organizations reporting bad news is career limiting so the project performance is massaged to show an optimistic picture: however the truth will emerge sooner or later and somebody is going to need to deal with it then. I know of a case where they closed the project and called it a success even though it is not. An example is a Sponsor telling the Project Manager to change the performance status indicator from Red to Green.)

5. We need more controls. This will involve more regular reporting by the Project Manager and may require external audits.

   (*Comment* - While more controls might provide some level of comfort to the Governance body, this extra work distracts from ongoing project work and ultimately its performance, so be careful in this situation.)

6. Provide more "support". This support may be extra or different resources, advice, extension of time or budget, speedier decision-making etc.

   (*Comment* - This assumes we understand what the problem is. If we do not know what the problem source is, providing more support may simply delay the real solution while spending more money unnecessarily.)

7. Understand the root cause of the problem and whether it can be fixed. There are many possible reasons including:
   - Original estimates were unrealistic;
   - The scope of work was incomplete, unclear or very volatile due to changes of mind or direction. Or it could be all of the above;
   - Inappropriate resources applied as they were the only ones available;
   - What is being attempted is more complex than originally imagined and this was not considered in the risk identification and planning.
   - Governance body not operating effectively and making speedy decisions on critical matters.

   The cause may be a combination of above. It is rarely one issue.

   (*Comment* - It may be necessary to find someone independent to discover the root cause as the program or project team may be too close to the action and also too busy doing the work. In one case the Governance body stopped the project for 3 months while they re-planned it, a very brave but correct action to take, and which ultimately proved successful. Finding root cause is not easy and may take some time and expertise but is worth it in the long run.)

Ultimately it is about facing up to reality, and the sooner we discover what that reality is, the more likely the corrective action can be taken successfully. Delays simply limit the potential for a range of future corrective actions. While we do not want to react too soon, we also do not want to lose opportunities to make the appropriate change. Experience tends to show that we leave it longer than we should before taking effective action, but then hindsight is a wonderful teacher.

Several quotes that I think really need to be considered carefully. These come from a document called "100 rules for NASA Project Managers", which you can easily find on the Internet by searching.

"All problems are solvable in time, so make sure that you have enough schedule contingency – if you don't the next project manager that takes your place will."

"Mistakes are all right but failure is not. Failure is just mistakes you can't recover from; therefore, try and create contingency plans or alternate approaches for the items or plans that have high risk. "

However, it usually takes several failures before people (both PMs and Governance bodies) begin to recognize the need for adequate contingency and realistic schedules and budgets.

Author

Harold Ainsworth has held senior management positions in several project service organizations involving oversight of large complex projects, and been responsible for several organization change management initiatives. Also he has considerable experience as a consultant and educator in portfolio, program and project management in both Australia and South East Asia. His current consulting work is in helping organizations achieve sustainable value from their strategic investments through effective Governance, and the practices of portfolio, program and project management.

Harold holds post-graduate qualifications in management and is a member of four professional organizations, and he teaches part-time at two Australian Universities in their graduate Project Management Programs.

www.ingramcontent.com/pod-product-compliance
Lightning Source LLC
Chambersburg PA
CBHW071114210326
41519CB00020B/6289